WHEN ALL ELSE FAILS, HIRE A FUNDRAISER

A practical guide
to raising money for your cause

Cindy Stanleigh

WHEN ALL ELSE FAILS, HIRE A FUNDRAISER

_____

Cindy Stanleigh

STANLEIGH PRESS   TORONTO
WHEN ALL ELSE FAILS, HIRE A FUNDRAISER

For information
STANLEIGH PRESS,
978-0-9937971
Toronto, Ontario
www.stanleighpress.com

ISBN   978-0-9937971-1-8
ISBN(e-book)   978-0-9937971-0-1
First Edition: OCTOBER 2014
10 9 8 7 6 5 4 3 2 1

About the Author

For the past twenty years, Cindy Stanleigh has helped several charitable organizations raise millions of dollars. All of these charities faced a range of complex funding challenges. Using a pragmatic, creative approach, Stanleigh helped these organizations raise funds, diversify income channels, and strengthen operational goals. Having worked as a Grants Officer for private foundations, after reviewing thousands of grant applications, Stanleigh also understands the philanthropic world from the viewpoint of the funder.

This book will demystify the fundraising process and provide you with solid, realistic, proven strategies to help your organization raise funds right away. If you are looking for help without the hype, and if you have a positive attitude, this book is for you.

To David:

Thanks for travelling down this path by my side and thanks for all the fish!

CONTENTS

"I shall pass this way but once; any good, therefore, that I can do or any kindness that I can show to any human being, let me do it now. Let me not defer nor neglect it, for I shall not pass this way again."

Etienne de Grellet

Chapter 1

'IT TAKES A VILLAGE' TO RAISE THE FUNDS YOU NEED

I've worked with hundreds of colleagues, volunteers, and friends over the years in an effort to raise funds for a variety of charities. Don't worry: raising funds really isn't difficult. It takes courage, perseverance, and compassion to approach others for funds; however, the act of giving is a powerful, positive human experience. In fact, according to a recent study entitled "Spending Money on Others Promotes Happiness," published by Harvard Business School and the Department of Psychology at the University of British Columbia (Dunn, Aknin & Norton),

"participants who were randomly assigned to spend money on others experienced greater happiness than those assigned to spend money on themselves."

Once you recognize that others want to contribute to helping make this world a better place, you will see that the door of funding opportunity is just waiting for you to open it.

Here are some factors to consider before you begin your journey:

Basic objective
Why does this charity need to raise funds?

Ambition
Do you want the charity to succeed? How do you define success?

Perseverance
Are you willing to drive around any obstacles that come your way? (There will be some; I guarantee it!)

Passion
Do you feel passionate about what the charity does?

A great team
Is everyone involved in the organization part of a team, or have some factions developed along the way?

Outreach and networking
Do friends, colleagues, family members know about the value of this charitable work?

Collaboration
Have collaborative opportunities been considered? Are there companies, other charities or community organizations that are willing to help out?

Communication
Is the charity's mission and vision statement well defined?

Strategy
Have short and long-term strategies been planned?

Reflection
Does the organization review its mandate at least once a year?

Diversity
Does the organization attract diverse support?

Energy

If your team is feeling exhausted, have you considered strategies that will ignite your work?

Problem Solving

Has your team built in systems to solve problems that arise?

Focus and comparative analysis

Are other organizations duplicating your work? Can you learn from the success of other organizations?

Creativity

Can your term supply a creative approach to solving challenges?

Succession

What would you do if key team members left the organization?

Do you work or volunteer for a charity? I'm sure you passionately believe this charity contributes to the world in a valuable way. You have committed your precious time to this charity, which now needs to raise more money.

Perhaps the charity wants to improve staff salaries or is launching a capital campaign for a new research center or to renovate existing premises; perhaps the charity wants to increase the research budget or expand operational programs. Most likely, the funding strategies of the past no longer work as well as they used to and operational funding is weakening. Whether you're in charge of raising funds or you simply want to contribute to your team's efforts, I hope this book will help you achieve your goals. This book will help you develop a realistic, creative strategy and clarify how you can raise more money with or without the help of a fundraising professional.

This book is written from a Canadian perspective and the statistical information is Canadian; however, the general concepts will apply in most fundraising environments.

In many cases, those with whom I worked were aware of only a small part of what I did. This is because fundraising is a fairly comprehensive field encompassing a diverse range of activities and skills.

You don't have to possess all of these skills if you can find volunteers with a range of abilities to assist you through your fundraising journey.

A professional fundraiser is expected to be knowledgeable in the areas of event management, marketing, writing, volunteer coordination, database analysis, social networking and integration, communications, financial reporting, and more.

In short, a professional fundraiser is often a multitalented, multitasking individual with the diverse skills and expertise needed to succeed.

Below is a list of some of the many tasks a professional fundraiser is expected to execute. However, understand that this job description is not static. External and internal factors and needs will influence the job description for your charity. Among other considerations, your organization will need to factor in its size, both overall and within the development department—if it has one. As you can imagine, most fund development positions require a solid commitment of time to accomplish these typical tasks:

- Educate staff and volunteers about fundraising techniques and laws impacting charitable fundraising

- Manage administrative systems related to fundraising (database systems, internet giving systems, accounting systems, communications systems, website integration, relationship management systems, event administration, and web systems)

- Organize and recruit volunteers

- Organize, conceptualize, and manage all aspects of fundraising events

- Author and coordinate direct mail campaign (traditional and electronic)

- Hire direct mail company if not organized in-house

- Integrate social media, direct mail, event, and email campaigns

- Manage communications, including the development of key messages, to ensure that all internal and external messages are consistent

- Author and research prospective government, corporate, and foundation proposals

- Manage processes related to stewardship practices (keeping donors engaged and ensure gifts are renewed and grown)

- Manage telephone solicitation program if implemented

- Manage major gift solicitation campaign

- Manage Planned Giving initiatives (print and web materials, personal visits, volunteer training)

- Manage online giving portal, peer-to-peer campaigns, e-campaigns, newsletter distribution

- Make recommendations and report results on an ongoing basis

- Hire or lead strategic planning sessions related to development practices with enthusiasm

- Liaise with directors and/or fund development volunteers

- Liaise with staff/manage administrative staff.

Contrary to popular belief, raising funds doesn't require the use of secret information, magic wands, or special incantations.

Creative solutions to your charity's financial problems do exist and these solutions are often discovered by building a network of passionate, enthusiastic, AND creative 'champions' who are willing to work and will share their contacts, thoughts, time, and ideas.

Fundraising is a team effort, not a solitary activity.

This fact may disturb the team members who would rather not participate in fundraising initiatives. Your organization's leaders will be disappointed if they believe they can just hire a fundraiser and expect the funds will roll in without any involvement required by the Board itself. Without a great team, you won't reach your fundraising goals. A small team will not be as effective as a big team. The math is simple.

I'm providing you with a basic recipe for fundraising. Your success will be limited—I guarantee it—if your 'champions,' both paid staff and volunteers, do not have these qualities:

Recipe for a great fundraising strategy

- Passionate interest in and support of the organization's mission and vision by all directors, staff, and participants in the fundraising process.

- A thorough understanding of what your organization does and why it exists.

- A specific understanding of why the organization needs to raise funds.

- The ability to focus, persevere and communicate to others about the mission and vision of the organization.

- Willingness to follow through with

consistent energy and enthusiasm.

If your organization is considering hiring a professional fundraiser, please consider this book's suggestions before you start the process. Information can help you overcome inexperience.

Here is a list of *inappropriate* questions to ask:

"We don't have any money; will you work on commission?"

Professional fundraising associations do not allow members to work on commission. Here's an analogy to compare this offer with that of a private sector offer for a manager or executive:

"Our share prices are down, our cash flow is limited, and our products are in competition with 20,000 other companies that produce the same product; are you willing to work on commission?"

"We would like you to raise money for us. How much do you charge?"

Does anyone walk into a job interview expecting the organization to have absolutely no idea of how much they are willing to pay the individual?   There are many resources available to indicate current salary expectations of professional candidates. Make sure to do some research before you meet with a potential candidate.

"We would like to double our funding this year. If we hire you, how will you achieve this goal?"

The fundraiser will not achieve this goal alone, and if you think he/she will, you will be disappointed. No doubt, there are consultants who will make promises they cannot keep. I've reviewed plenty of charitable fundraising advertisements asking for a fundraiser who will help their organization increase revenue. Many of these charities don't have a proper strategic plan in place, nor do they have a robust marketing, administrative, or fundraising budget. If these are your circumstances, how realistic are your expectations?

"If everyone is moving forward together, then success takes care of itself."

Henry Ford

Chapter 2

COLLABORATION IS THE SECRET WEAPON

Consider for a moment that your organization operates like a sports team. As soon as the players cease to perform properly, your team will lose the game. This situation applies to charities in the same way. If your charity exhibits serious operational deficiencies and/or unenthusiastic or dysfunctional personnel (staff and/or volunteers), the charity's success will be limited. Team spirit is of primary concern when beginning to make positive changes. Positive collaboration isn't an option; it is the key to success.

During my career, I have met with volunteers from charitable organizations who claim to have an urgent need for more funds and think hiring a fundraiser is the solution to their funding challenges. When probed for their expectations, they assume the fundraiser will write some grants, talk to a few people, and the money will flow in without any effort on their part.

I have worked with fundraising 'superheros' who make promises to "take the organization to the next level" by raising generous amounts of funds. The board or fundraising committee is often discouraged and disappointed with poor results from this type of consultant because they make unrealistic promises they can't keep.

Fundraising personnel and consultants burn out quickly and move on to the next fund development position after an average of 16 to 18 months. If the organization is trying to raise funds and isn't succeeding, there are reasons—whether it's organizational dysfunction, unrealistic expectations, an incompetent fundraiser, or some other problem—it's easy to play the blame game. Lack of collaborative strategic effort is often the reason for fundraising failure.

A single individual doesn't produce every fundraising dollar any more than a private company's revenue depends on one salesperson. If a product or service is of poor quality, or if the executive hasn't led the company well, the organization will not succeed. A corporation can hire the best salesperson in the world to sell its products, but that person's efforts can't make the company succeed if the delivery of products or services doesn't represent the quality promised during the sales pitch or in marketing materials.

You might assume that the work your charity does is so wonderful that people are waiting around the corner with a hole burning through their wallets to support this great work. You imagine that the expensive, well-established fundraiser can find those special people who are just waiting to be asked for a donation. This superhero fundraiser will elicit a sense of confidence in the charitable work, and the coveted multimillion-dollar check we all read about in the newspaper will be delivered to your charity's door. This is a common assumption: that "the fundraiser will fix this" so that all financial challenges are removed.

"Do, or do not. There is no try."
Yoda

Chapter 3

THE MULTI-MILLION DOLLAR DONATION

You keep reading about it, don't you? You read about a multi-million dollar donation in the newspaper just the other day. Here's the truth. A huge donation does not appear overnight. It is mostly the result of a long-term, strategic, well-placed plan using personal and profound connections to a cause. This relationship nearly always takes years to blossom into a huge gift to the charity. Further, in approximately 80 percent of these cases, the big gifts go to the wealthiest 20th percent of charitable organizations.

Some organizations want to hire a fundraiser and haven't the funds to pay for one. This situation is typical of organizations that want fundraisers to work on a commission basis. The Association of Fundraising Professionals has a code of ethics that strictly prohibits professional fundraisers from acquiring payment on a commission basis for good reason.

Hiring a fundraiser is like hiring an orchestra conductor. The fundraiser can help the orchestra work together, but the fundraiser can't play every instrument in the orchestra at the same time. Fund development depends on enthusiastic paid and volunteer resources and includes a well-thought-out strategy that encompasses every level of operational activity.

Fundraising doesn't happen in a day, but your group can start working on various tasks immediately.

Before I discuss strategy, you should consider the emotional/psychological side of fundraising. Without an understanding of emotional factors, your strategies will not work as well as they should.

With a positive attitude, some creative energy, some knowledge under your belt, and a great, enthusiastic team, your organization will raise the funds it needs.

"Become the change you wish to see in the world."

Gandhi

Chapter 4

WHAT EXACTLY IS A CHARITY?

Much of the following information is important but is not commonly known; it is drawn from the website of the Canadian Centre for Philanthropy, a research organization dedicated to monitoring the charitable and not-for-profit sector in Canada.

A registered charity as defined by Revenue Canada is:

"An organization established and operated for charitable purposes, and [it] must devote its resources to charitable activities. The charity must be resident in Canada, and cannot use its income to benefit its members."

A charity also has to meet a public benefit test. To qualify under this test, an organization must show that:

• its activities and purposes provide a tangible benefit to the public

- those people who are eligible for benefits are either the public as a whole, or a significant section of it, in that they are not a restricted group or one where members share a private connection, such as social clubs or professional associations with specific membership

- the charity's activities are legal and are not contrary to public policy

To register as a charity, the organization has to be either incorporated or governed by a legal document called a trust or a constitution. This document has to explain the organization's purposes and structure.

For more information on Revenue Canada's definition of a charity and tax related issues regarding registered charities, go to:

http://www.cra-arc.gc.ca

Competition in the sector

Many people are surprised by how competitive the charitable sector is. The top 1 percent (hospitals, universities, colleges) of organizations command 60 percent of all revenues.

- There are an estimated 161,000 nonprofits and charities in Canada.

- About 85,000 of these are registered charities (recognized by the Canada Revenue Agency).

- The sector represents $106 billion or 7.1 percent of the Gross Domestic Product (larger than the automotive or manufacturing industries).

Where does the money come from?

In a 2009 Statistics Canada report entitled "The Satellite Account of Nonprofit Institutions and Volunteering," a surprising list of facts summarizing where the revenue came from was outlined:

- sales of goods and services account for 45.6 percent of total income

- government funding, 19.7 percent

- membership fees, 15.9 percent

- donations from households, 12.0 percent

- investment income, 4.9 percent

If you love examining the charitable sector, you should visit the Imagine Canada website where current reporting, sector initiatives, and research studies are published. The website address is: www.imaginecanada.ca

With almost 10 times the population of Canada, the U.S. naturally boasts much higher charitable numbers. According to the website of the National Center for Charitable Statistics (2013), the United States has 1,537,465 tax-exempt organizations. Some 955,817 are defined as public charities, and 97,792 are considered private foundations. There are 483,856 other types of nonprofit organizations, including chambers of commerce, fraternal organizations, and civic leagues.

Other juicy facts outline that in 2010, nonprofits accounted for **9.2 percent of all wages and salaries** paid in the United States. (Source: The Nonprofit Almanac, 2012)

United States public charity finances

According to NCCS Core Files 2011, public charities reported over **$1.59 trillion in total revenues and $1.49 trillion in total expenses. Of the revenue:**

- 22 percent came from contributions, gifts, and government grants

- 72 percent came from program service revenues, which include government fees and contracts

- 6 percent came from 'other' sources

including dues, rental income, special event income, and gains from goods sold

According to Giving USA, 2012, charitable contributions by individuals, foundations, bequests, and corporations reached $298.42 billion in 2011, an increase of 0.9 percent from the revised 2010 estimates and after adjusting for inflation. Of these charitable contributions:

• Religious organizations received almost a third, and the largest share, with 32 percent of total estimated contributions.

• Educational institutions received the second largest percentage, with 13 percent of total estimated contributions.

• Human service organizations accounted for 12 percent of total estimated contributions in 2010, the third largest share.

• According to The Foundation Center, 2012, foundations gave $46.9 billion in 2011, up 2.2 percent from 2010. Of total foundation giving in 2010:

• 71 percent came from independent foundations

• 9 percent came from community foundations

• 11 percent came from corporate

foundations

- 9 percent came from operating foundations

"To conquer fear is the beginning of wisdom."

Bertrand Russell

Chapter 5

EVERYONE HATES FUNDRAISING

Your organization wants to raise more funds. To find out how others feel about fundraising in your organization, try this quick and easy exercise. Ask your volunteers, directors, and staff to write down every adjective or idea that comes to mind when they think of the word 'fundraising.'

Here are some typical answers I have received from participants who engaged in this exercise:

- **scary**
- **frightening**
- **humiliating**
- **horrible**
- **embarrassing**
- **unfortunate**

- **something someone else should do**
- **not my cup of tea**
- **annoying**
- **difficult**
- **aggressive**

Can you imagine how I feel when I see these answers? After all, I have been 'fundraising' for more than twenty years, and when each day of fundraising comes to a close, this isn't how I feel at all. In fact, fundraising can be exhilarating and rewarding. Think of how wonderful you will feel when you and your colleagues have solved some of your most challenging financial challenges.

Our choices reflect our values. We as humans spend money on three things:

- what we need
- what we desire
- what we believe in

When you agree to fundraise on behalf of a charitable organization, you will undertake the task of asking others to invest in something beyond their own personal needs. People donate to charities because it makes them feel good and because they feel a connection with the vision and mission of the charity.

You can feel positive about approaching potential donors if you are genuine and sincere about what you are asking the prospective donor to support.

After all, you will not benefit personally from donations. You are asking people to donate to a worthwhile cause. You needn't worry about how they will feel or how they will respond to your request. You will receive one of two answers: Yes or No. As long as you have prepared your proposal (verbal and written) in a positive, sincere manner, the answer will not depend on your approach or your work; it will depend on the values, needs, and desires of the prospective donor.

Focus on discussing how important the charity is from your point of view (using the mission, vision statement, and key messages). Ask that the prospective donor consider your point of view. If possible, make a connection between the charity and the individual receiving your appeal. For example, if your charity helps homeless teens, ask questions such as: "Have you ever wondered about how a homeless teen ends up on the street?" "Did you ever think of leaving home when you were a teen?"

Talk about why you are involved with the organization and how connected you feel to the charity. If the individual you have approached is interested, that person will embrace the idea; if they are not interested, you can change the discussion to whatever else is on your mind and make the meeting an enjoyable opportunity for some social time.

No matter what you say, remember to:

- Give the potential donor an opportunity to speak

- Listen closely to what the potential donor says

- Look for common ground

Using your understanding of your potential donor's life experiences, search for why your charity might be of interest to the donor. Try to direct limited focus to yourself and focus the discussion on the potential donor. Try to find some common ground.

Here are some of the basic universal rules of fundraising to consider:

You must ask for a donation.

When was the last time you woke up in the morning and asked yourself, "Is today a good day to help the homeless with a donation?"

You might deeply care about those who are homeless, sick, or hungry, but you are unlikely to make a donation to a charity unless you are prompted to do so. If your organization doesn't ask for a donation, it won't receive one. When asking for a donation, here are some tips to keep in mind:

• **Suggest a specific amount;** a suggested amount of money is an essential factor in this equation.

• **Suggest a higher amount;** you will receive more funds than if you asked for less (more on this later).

• **Tell the potential donor,** in specific terms, what accomplishments their donation will enable; give your donor the opportunity to feed a street youth for a month for $250 or to purchase a wheelchair for $1,000.

Personalize your dialogue.

People give to people. If your friends or neighbors ask you to support a cause that truly means something to them, you are more likely to make a donation than if you are approached by a stranger with the same request. One's emotional connection to the person asking for a donation motivates them to feel the spirit of generosity. People don't donate to institutions; they think about themselves and their personal commitments or needs and their attachment to causes, concerns, and situations close to their hearts. People give with their hearts and not with their heads.

When talking to each prospective donor, try to visualize how that person will think and feel about the work you are doing. Find a common thread that will let you weave your case or mission into the conversation. Your donor will want to give if:

a) the cause seems worth the investment in time and/or money and

b) trusted acquaintances have also given.

People who donate are happier.

Think about the last time you gave someone a special gift. Didn't it feel great to give something that person loved? Many studies show that giving feels good, and frankly, it makes a whole lot of sense.

While asking for a donation, describe how wonderful the donor will feel when he/she relieves hunger, supports an artistic endeavor, helps endangered species, provides services to those in need, or contributes to curing diseases. Everyone wants to help make the world a better place in some way. You can show your donors that they can play an active role by contributing to your cause.

Make it easy.

Offer every possible method for making that donation: cash, checks, Visa, MasterCard, American Express, via the internet, in person, or through the mail in a pre-addressed and stamped envelope... in every way possible to facilitate ease of giving. Remove reasons for not giving, and donors will be more likely to give.

Don't despair if prospects say no.

I don't want to discourage you, but you will not always be successful. Don't despair if your potential donor rejects your proposal. When a prospective donor says yes, you will celebrate even more enthusiastically. Learning how to take rejection is an essential skill for fundraisers. Remember that a rejection today doesn't necessarily mean a rejection tomorrow. Persevere. Most importantly, don't take the rejection personally.

"I like the dreams of the future better than the history of the past."

Thomas Jefferson

Chapter 6

WHY DO YOU WANT TO RAISE MORE MONEY?

This is the first question I ask an organization that requests fundraising assistance. During meetings with an organization's leaders, I am not always convinced that the charity needs to raise its level of funding. Often, the charitable board of directors may get caught up in the profit-driven psychology of the private sector.

This 'need for growth' doesn't always paint a practical, realistic picture in the charitable sector. Sometimes there is room for growth; sometimes there is an increased need for the charitable organization to grow. However, before significantly increasing your charitable budget, make sure there are compelling reasons to grow. Make sure your work isn't being duplicated by another charity before engaging in a growth strategy. Your organization might consider cooperative or amalgamated work.

Consider the list below. I have enumerated good reasons to raise more funds and listed some not so good reasons to raise more funds.

Here are some good reasons to increase funding:

• Staff members are poorly paid or are due for raises (however, this lacks fundraising appeal).

• Operational costs have increased over the years.

• Capital improvements are necessary.

• More funds are needed to continue important medical research.

• The demand/need for a social service has increased.

• More students need help from a scholarship fund.

• The organization currently has an operating deficit.

• The organization has lost a major funding source. This signals a need to diversify your revenue strategy.

• A sudden relevant global crisis that

requires immediate attention.

Avoid these reasons to increase fundraising goals:

- Because other charities are raising more money than we do.

- Because we attended a terrific fundraising event that another charity coordinated, and I think we can do this too.

- Because there are lots of wealthy people out there who just haven't heard about how wonderful we are.

- Although we don't have a specific operational goal, we would like to expand our programs because it seems like the right thing to do.

- Because we keep reading about other charities that are raising millions of dollars.

- Because I'm on a committee of another charity, and they are raising a lot more money than this one does.

"I have seen the future, and it works."
Lincoln Steffens

Chapter 7

BUDGETING FOR SUCCESS

Some of the organizations I have worked with don't have a formal budget planning ritual. Budgets are really important because they spell out exactly where the money raised will be spent. More importantly, the budget will help the fundraising committee and fundraiser determine how much money they need to raise. The budget provides your group with the basis for a fundraising strategy.

Since individuals and organizations like to bring a tangible benefit to the charity, many of the donation levels are categorized. For example, a donor can sponsor a child, purchase a van or hospital bed, feed a village, purchase a life-saving water well, and more.

The staff and board of directors of every charity must develop and approve a budget yearly. This annual budget is your funding template, guiding the staff and volunteers toward specific goals. It is important to be clear about how much money is needed and how it will be spent. The budget should be realistic and reflect the charity's priorities. Gaining this clarity is an important part of the process and helps your organization focus on measurable revenue goals.

Raising funds for the purpose of raising funds is not going to resonate with prospective donors. Your charity will succeed if a clear message/need/vision is delivered to your prospective donors and sponsors.

Remember to consider that the budget is a guideline. There is no guarantee that the revenue stream and the expenses will not be modified throughout the year. Any significant purchases not preapproved during the budgetary process can be submitted for director approval before the purchase takes place.

Capital improvements (buildings, vans, major pieces of equipment) are often categorized separately from the 'operating' budget of the charity.

"Though you drive away nature with a pitchfork, she always returns."

Horace

Chapter 8

THE PARETO PRINCIPLE

Have you heard of the Pareto Principle? This principle applies to every organization in both the profitable and nonprofit sectors and appears to describe a rule of nature. In its broadest sense, the rule applies to uneven distribution of resources; business consultant Joseph Juran named it after the Italian economist who observed that 80 percent of Italy's land was owned by 20 percent of its people. Understanding this rule can help you and your organization work smarter, not harder, so that you put most of your efforts where it really counts and eliminate activities that don't produce results.

How might this simple rule apply to your nonprofit? It could mean that:

•   80 percent of contributions come from 20 percent of donors

- 80 percent of volunteer hours are contributed by 20 percent of volunteers

- 80 percent of the work is done by 20 percent of the staff

To take advantage of this rule, between 60 and 80 percent of your efforts should be concentrated on revenue coming from the top 20 percent of your revenue sources. You can strategically plan how you would deal with the loss of those top donors or workers, because this rule can identify where your organization is vulnerable as well as where effort should be directed.

I was once hired by an organization that had been receiving 80 percent of its revenue from one source, an annual $200,000 corporate donation. The retirement of the company's CEO, who had championed the donation, resulted in the entire donation being cancelled without warning. Fortunately, the organization had a contingency fund to handle the transition to a different funding model. In many cases, diversification of funding sources can help your organization maintain a healthy income. If your organization has limited resources, a strategic fund development plan can help you focus your efforts. It is easy to get sidetracked by a variety of possible opportunities that may arrive at your doorstep.

"Whatever is worth doing at all is worth doing well."

Earl of Chesterfield, 1746

Chapter 9

STEWARDSHIP AND THE ART OF BEING GRATEFUL

In my experience, stewardship is often considered to be a policy issue. Good stewardship can be achieved by showing your donors that you are sincerely grateful. This process begins by producing a policy document for approval by the board of directors and ends with numerous acts of gratitude and appreciation.

In the charitable sector, stewardship refers to the activities culminating from the receipt of a gift. The procedures outlined in your stewardship policy will define how your organization will show appreciation and gratitude for the gift(s) received from a donor.

These procedures should be valued, with regular rituals and relationship building honored. Showing a sincere appreciation for the gifts your organization has received will result in an increase in those gifts and feelings of goodwill as well.

Mistakes and careless handling of a donor's gift(s) can be exponentially damaging.

Here's a real-life example using generic names to show what can happen if a gift is not appreciated and a stewardship policy is ignored:

ABC Charity sends out a letter and brochure asking large companies to sponsor a charity event. Smith Corporation agrees, sending a $1,000 check. The administrative assistant at ABC Charity puts the donation aside among a pile of papers and forgets about it. The fundraiser had been told that the donation had been received, but it doesn't appear on a database report summarizing the sponsors of the charity event.

The fundraiser asks what happened to Smith Corporation's check, but no one else remembers that the charity received it. One month later, the administrative assistant finds the Smith Corporation donation while sorting paperwork. The Smith Corporation receives a thank-you letter and a receipt more than a month after sending the donation and never makes another donation to this charity.

Everyone involved in every organization can make a difference when it comes to fundraising. This rule includes the individual who answers the phone and greets people at the door. Every person in the organization plays a relevant role in the fund development process; I can't emphasize this enough.

Everyone who talks about the charity, works with that charity, and visualizes its future can and will affect its financial bottom line. Make sure that all players realize that the charity's existence depends on each person's capacity to encourage others to support the cause.

Your organization should compose a stewardship policy; many examples can be found online. However, you will waste time and paper if you simply adopt a policy without implementing it.

Here are some highlights of what a stewardship policy should contain:

- Who will record the gift information?

- What is the timeline for recording the receipt of the gift?

- Who records and processes payments?

- Where is the record of the donation stored (database program, paper files)?

- Who will thank the donor?

- Who will compose the letter of thanks?

If a gift is a major gift (your organization should determine what level of gift is considered 'major'), a personal phone call should be made by either a senior staff member (good idea) or a volunteer director (better idea) or a volunteer who has had a personal connection to the charitable cause and may have benefited from the gift (only when appropriate).

Always make sure that the gift is acknowledged as promised—whether such recognition is in newsletters, on web pages, at events, in programs, on plaques, or all of those.

If you ignore your donors or treat them without the utmost respect, you will lose their support—guaranteed. Treat your donors as if they are a part of the family. They care about your work, but it is easy to take them for granted. If you neglect your donors, your organization will lose valuable financial support.

"The secret is to gang up on the problem, rather than each other."

Thomas Stallkamp

Chapter 10

GANG UP ON THE PROBLEM

Without collaboration, your organization will walk down a frustrating and dysfunctional path. Walk down every path with positive enthusiasm and you will succeed!

Whenever you see any sign of factional behavior in your organization, remind all involved that they are there to serve the mission and vision of the organization. The volunteer board of directors of a charitable organization has a fiduciary (legal) responsibility to ensure the charity is run in a respectful, professional manner. To ensure the smooth operation of a charity, the board and staff must work as an enthusiastic team at every level.

More specifically, if members of the board of directors perceive themselves as a senior management team without the need for input from the staff they hired to run, the charitable organization could begin to lose revenue, spirit, passion, and opportunities, while being pre-occupied with the destructive force of ego-driven behaviors.

Make every effort to avoid these behaviors. I've seen it too often, and it can derail the organization's mission and vision. The charitable sector provides a rare opportunity for our society to create, without profit, organizations that exist purely for the greater good.

When individuals in an organization work together as a positive team, the charity is likely to thrive. Solve problems together as a team and include every player. The challenges your organization faces will not be solved using factional decision making processes. It never works. Collaboration is a crucial key to success.

"A goal without an action plan is a daydream."

Nathaniel Brandon

Chapter 11

TIME TO DREAM - THE STRATEGIC PLAN

To plan your organization's future consider engaging in a formal strategic planning process.

An experienced, professional facilitator should lead the strategic planning process. This facilitator should be able to gather and assess ideas, thoughts, and strategies and to assist with the development and adoption of the final plan. This individual must be completely objective; to avoid having biased ideas, the facilitator should not be working with or on the board of directors nor as a staff member of the organization. It is critical to find someone who is completely neutral.

If you work with a national organization with many chapters, the best time to hold a strategic planning session is during a general meeting of members, so that as many representatives of your organization as possible can be included. The more the merrier in this case.

A strategic plan is not an option; it is a necessity. Creating the plan, however, is just the first step; the plan must then be implemented, with the strategy reviewed quarterly. Review and amend your strategic plan every two or three years. A strategic planning session should accompany this biannual process of review.

The strategic planning process allows your team (volunteer and paid staff) to collaboratively put a solid, successful organizational system in place. If managed properly, the strategic planning meeting will allow every participant to feel valued. Throw away hierarchical concepts during this process. The strategic planning session should be fun, casual, engaging, energetic, creatively managed, and sincerely implemented with positive intent.

Here is a basic planning guide for the process your group will accomplish:

What: Schedule a brainstorming session to precisely identify the organization's mission and to establish a strategy to fulfill the mission and accomplish the goals.

Who: Invite all volunteer directors and all staff (whenever possible); stress the importance of attending this important planning session.

Why: When everyone's opinion and input is considered and valued, those involved in implementing and monitoring the plan will fully endorse it.

Where: Find a place that provides comfort and nurtures creativity. The physical environment of the meeting place is important. Those participating should feel relaxed and inspired. Participants will find it easier to visualize a positive outcome if they are physically comfortable. Ensure that your meeting space supports this process. The space should be visually appealing; avoid an ugly, bland, windowless meeting room with glaring fluorescent or artificial lighting. Encourage participants to dress comfortably and casually. Seek a quiet, inspiring environment. This meeting is not the place to require appropriate workplace attire, nor is it meant to be a formal event. It is a creative brainstorming session.

When: Schedule this process as soon as possible, while considering the need to include as many staff and volunteers as possible. The meeting should not take more than six hours, and meals and snacks should be available to all participants. If your organization doesn't have the resources to order food, you can consider a potluck format. Your organization should repeat and review this process at least once every two to three years.

Strategic Planning Meeting Structure:

Welcome (15 minutes to half hour)

Welcome everyone to the meeting and establish that the task before participants is a creative process, without rules or right answers. The first activity is to ask all participants to introduce themselves and talk about how they became involved with the charity and what the charity means to them on a personal level. After introductions, distribute a copy of the agenda. Make sure everyone has supplies for taking notes.

The Mission (approximately one hour)

If you already have a mission statement, the facilitator should write it on the white/black board for all to see and discuss. Each participant is asked if there is anything he or she would add to or change in the mission statement. The facilitator should either collect comments on sticky notes or write the ideas on the board for all participants to see. After the meeting, the facilitator will help the group compose or improve the mission statement— a brief, comprehensive paragraph that can be used in all printed and electronic communications materials. The mission statement defines the reason your organization exists and is worthy of support from others. Make sure the mission statement is brief, memorable, passionate, and clear.

Once all ideas have been discussed, proceed to the next step. The moderator/facilitator will take all notes and review and compose the final mission statement for board approval at a later date.

Key Messages:

Every individual perceives the organization differently and expresses his or her definition of the mission and vision of the organization differently. Key messages are developed to deliver consistent communication to the outside world. Brainstorming ideas that are recorded and collected during the strategic planning session could likely be quite lengthy and comprehensive and can be used for more than just refining a mission statement. The facilitator or a communications specialist can collect and review these ideas and compose a comprehensive list of key messages. Key messages should be written down and delivered to everyone involved with the organization because they ensure that all communications messages are consistent with the mission and vision of the organization.

Key messages should be consistently quoted on all materials (electronic and printed materials). Every media release and conversation with prospective donors, sponsors, or media personnel should refer to these messages. Key messages are your 'pitch,' your soul, describe your mission, your reason for being, words that clearly describe your purpose and drive an emotional response. Key messages are more comprehensive than the mission statement paragraph. These messages deliver important detailed information to prospective donors and other interested parties.

The Vision (approximately one hour)

This portion of the meeting focuses on the participants' ability to dream about the future. The time span you should focus on is the time span between this meeting and your next strategic planning meeting (ideally, two years from now). The question posed to the planning committee is, where would you like to see the organization two years from now?

Do you want to expand your programs, build new buildings, eradicate your debt, increase your research program, provide staff with better pay, and enhance your capacity to provide services to your constituency?

Each participant should have an opportunity to talk about his or her vision, and all notes will be gathered and discussed with the group. If you use sticky notes, they can be placed at the front of the room for all to see. Your facilitator will summarize the results at a later date and compose a vision statement for review and approval by the board of directors.

The S.W.O.T. analysis (two hours)

A number of different systems can help you with strategic planning. For the purpose of this book, I will illustrate my own personal favorite, the S.W.O.T. analysis, developed by Albert Humphrey of the Stanford Research Institute. It is a clear, definitive system that encourages brainstorming and takes into account the full spectrum of possibilities. Here's how you can apply this methodology:

S = Strengths: Consider and list your organization's strengths. This might be the number of your members, the location of your charity, the number of stakeholders or constituents you have, the number of years you have operated, the reputation you have in your community, the number of people you serve, and the quality of your staff and volunteers. What is unique about your organization? What has your organization accomplished? What makes you stand out? Why do others support your work?

W = Weaknesses: List the aspects of your organization that need improvement. Some weaknesses might be internal (within the organization) and some of them might be external. For example, your administrative records are disorganized and you haven't had the resources to hire an administrator. Perhaps you don't have comfortable seats for your performances or you haven't kept up with the demand for your services. Perhaps you directly compete with other organizations. Your facilitator will ask all participants to list every weakness you can think of.

O = Opportunities: Are there opportunities you should be considering? Can you grow? Can you hire? Can you reorganize your systems? Can you merge or collaborate with other organizations? Are you close to solving a problem? Are you the only organization that does what you do? What is unique about your organization? Can you modify your funding model? Do you have talents that give you a monopoly?

T = Threats: Is your organization threatened with extinction? How many other organizations compete with your charity? Is there an internal struggle you haven't overcome? Is the need for your services diminishing? Are you too dependent on one major funding partner? Are you limited in how many people you can help?

Now that you have discussed nearly everything there is to discuss, the facilitator will ask the group to take another glance at the mission and vision statement and discuss whether these ideas need be amended. Solidify a series of goals that everyone can endorse. Examples of solidified goals include:

• **Diversify volunteer engagement** (find volunteers with specific skill sets that the organization needs, such as human resources, marketing, public relations, financial, and legal)

• **Form a committee** focused on a particular

goal (for instance, fundraising, public awareness, social media, web development, renovations)

- **Increase** member or donor **engagement**

- **Create** important policies (examples: Human Resources, Donor Stewardship, Financial Accountability, Building Design, Program Design)

Because all organizations are unique and their circumstances and needs are unique, I won't offer you a one-size-fits-all, comprehensive list of goals. Your facilitator will help guide your group through this process before the strategic planning meeting ends.

If a committee structure is established, it is important to set key dates for reporting on the development and implementation of each committee's activities.

The facilitator will collect all notes at the end of the meeting and then compose a final summary report that includes a proposed strategic plan based on the information collected during the meeting. If a strategic planning committee has been created, that committee would discuss the plan and forward a recommendation to the board of directors for final approval. Otherwise, the plan would go straight to the board for consideration. Once the plan has been adopted and initiated, the organization can begin to achieve its goals. This is the beginning of an important process, not the end. At the very least, this process will allow your organization to think about where it is now, where it wants to go, and how it will get there.

"Lose not yourself in a far off time, seize the moment that is thine."

Johann Friedrich Schiller

Chapter 12

KEEP YOUR EYE ON THE BALL

Strategic planning is effective only if the plan is implemented. Putting the plan into action might not work perfectly, especially at first, but I guarantee that if your organization doesn't implement the plan and monitor progress, it definitely won't be effective, and your charity will have wasted time and resources.

Your organization can address and correct or amend aspects of the strategy along the way and review progress during a series of follow-up meetings. You can consider setting up a committee that is responsible for monitoring the progress of the strategic plan. This will help keep everyone's eye on the ball.

Pay attention to the process after the plan is established and approved; otherwise, the plan is just a plan and nothing more. What good is that?

"One must learn by doing the thing; though you think you know it, you have no certainty until you try."

Sophocles

Chapter 13

PRACTICE MAKES PERFECT

I find fundraising exhilarating and rewarding but the average person working for a nonprofit finds asking for donations scary, embarrassing, and difficult.

Preparation and practice can change an excruciating experience to a positive one. To help persuade your staff and volunteers to approach others for a donation, you may need professional help. I suggest you hire a theatrical consulting group and conduct a workshop one afternoon or evening. The primary objective of this workshop is to practice asking for a donation from friends, family members, and colleagues. Why should you hire actors? Actors are masters of movement, voice, body expression, and presentation.

This workshop should incorporate telephone and in-person one-on-one techniques to allow volunteers and staff members to practice their approach and remove some of the emotional barriers that make approaching others difficult. Professional actors can help your group learn about body language, presentation skills, verbal and physical cues, and more. I suggest you conduct this workshop annually to refresh skills and nurture enthusiasm. In the public relations field, it is standard to practice the pitch before interviews by media personnel.

In the non-profit field, when staff members and volunteers have a chance to practice a pitch, they gain confidence, and the organization can be assured that everyone representing the nonprofit is conveying information accurately, consistently, and positively.

In summary, when preparing for a new fundraising drive, give your organization an opportunity to rehearse the 'ask' by using theatrical role-playing techniques.

"To send a letter is a good way to go somewhere without moving anything but your heart."

Phyllis Theroux

Chapter 14

DEAR FRIEND

Direct communication in the form of a letter, email, or text message is one of the first steps toward achieving your funding goals. This communication must be sincere, with consistent messaging. Techniques that will enhance your success include telling your story and writing your letter as if you were writing to your best friend.

A really strong letter is made up of a few essential ingredients:

- A compelling, emotional story

- Descriptive language to help the reader imagine the story

- Assurance that a donation will greatly benefit someone or something

- Two requests for a donation within the

text of the letter (the rule of thumb is to ask for a donation on the first page and in the last paragraph)

• A deadline to create a sense of urgency. Presenting a deadline—a 'call to action'— in the letter is important. This call to action encourages a quick response. If you don't incorporate a sense of urgency and call for a specific action within a stated timeline, potential donors might forget about your cause after they read the letter.

Suggest a 'due' date, e.g., "Please forward your payment before December 1st to give us enough time to purchase gifts for homeless people in our community."

Imagine that you are authoring a letter to a good friend. The story you tell has the power to transport your reader to another place. Just as a novel transports us to other realities, your direct mail letter should allow your potential donor to deeply understand your cause from an emotional point of view. Direct communication provides you with an opportunity to guide the reader and tell stories of who is helped by your organization and what it is accomplishing.

In the world of ephemeral electronic communications and distracted, overly busy people, your story and associated emotions might get lost if your message isn't strong. Your direct print or email communication presents an opportunity to change opinions and emotionally compel others to make a difference.

Review stories you read in magazines and in the newspaper. Which stories attract or move you? Why? Look at the language. Make sure to connect with your reader by adopting a strong cover line that will compel the reader to connect with your cause. Take advantage of attractive typography and use images that work symbiotically with the text. Some people respond better to images than to text, so always include visuals as well as words.

Direct mail is still an effective method of raising funds, contrary to what some people may believe. Direct mail is more tactile than electronic data; well-thought-out mailings help charities raise millions of dollars annually. People who complain about direct mail are usually incensed by the amount of 'wasted paper' involved in these campaigns.

The truth is, the reason why so many charities use direct mail to raise funds is because it works. It isn't always profitable enough, given the costs, but your charity can increase the likelihood of positive results by using very specific techniques. You won't necessarily be choosing to use direct mail instead of an electronic social media/email campaign. Direct mail and electronic communications should be combined into an effective integrated strategy.

Remember that every charity is different, its audience or constituency is different, and the results of every campaign will be different. The results of a direct mail campaign cannot be predicted accurately without first testing a variety of methods; however, I will share some tried and true rules associated with direct mail marketing.

Especially if you are short of funds, test a letter with a small segment of prospective donors to evaluate your strategy and investment.

If a test mailing to a small portion of your constituents succeeds, you will have evidence that your strategy is working, making it reasonable to spend money for a larger mailing.

There are two types of direct mail letters.

An appeal directed at someone who hasn't made a donation in the past. This person is commonly called a prospect in the fundraising world.

The other is a letter to an individual who has made a donation to the charity in the past. We will call this person a donor. If your charity's recordkeeping is in order, it should have an accurate, up-to-date list of supporters containing the following donor information:

- Name(s)
- Address(es)
- Phone numbers
- Email addresses

Without operational consistency to maintain accurate records, you will lose donors, insult donors, and/or send letters to nonexistent donors. I cannot emphasize enough that the accuracy of your database records is extremely important. If you send correspondence to nonexistent donors or insult them by getting their name wrong, you will lose funds.

Record additional information about the donor in the database for future use and reference:

- How were they introduced to the organization in the first place?
- What is their personal involvement in the

organization?

• When is their birthday? (You can send them a birthday card or e-card message to them in the future.)

• How much money have they donated in the past?

More tips on how to write an appeal to the donor:

• Make it personal.

• Dear Harold or Jennifer is better than Dear Friend.

• Use language that speaks directly to the donor.

• Refer to you more than to we. For example, don't write, "We will make sure that Johnny will find a safe foster home." Instead write: "Your past donation has helped us find a safe and caring foster home for Johnny."

• Be very clear about how the money will be used. I once received an email solicitation from a friend whose son was competing in a sporting competition. The appeal asked to support the team but the letter didn't provide me with a tangible reason for the financial request. Was the club purchasing new equipment? Did the cost of renting a sports field prohibit the club from operating in the future? Was the sports club providing scholarships to kids who couldn't afford to join the team? Unfortunately, this appeal didn't resonate with most of the recipients of the email and the campaign didn't reach its goal.

Personal stories resonate

We all relate to personal stories, while bare facts and figures fail to arouse emotion. One of my favorite videos demonstrates how powerful the personal storytelling experience can be. A meat grinder inserts an adorable piglet into a box under the sausage-making machine. Before the people see the piglet, they are quite content to eat the sausage, but when they make that personal connection, they are appalled. We identify with personal stories and experiences, not with information.

Remember to ask for a donation at least twice in each direct mail letter. Suggest a donation at the beginning of the letter and again at the end. If you don't ask for a donation, you probably won't get one.

For direct mail campaigns, make sure the appeal package contains a donation coupon that is really easy to complete, along with a self-addressed, stamped envelope. The easier it is for the individual to donate, the more likely the donation.

Providing an option for donating monthly may strengthen your relationship with your donor and make the donation more affordable, so you can widen your donor base. In the long term, monthly donors tend to be more loyal to the charity than those who give once a year. This is because the commitment is made on a regular basis.

Whenever possible, but especially when donations could be very significant, write letters by hand. If your database has 2,000 donors, writing all 2,000 letters by hand may not be a good use of your time. Recognizing the Pareto Principle, analyze your database. You likely will find that the top 20 percent of your donors gave more than 80 percent of your revenue. Keeping in mind the 80/20 rule, send handwritten letters to those individuals in the top 20 percent of donors. Because handwritten letters are more personal, they will mean a lot more to your most generous donors. Customize your message to each individual donor to add that personal touch.

To show the difference between an effective direct mail letter and an ineffective one, take a look at the following two letters. The first letter was unsuccessful. The second, while similar in intent, asks for a defined donation using a more personal approach. The second letter increased donations by 99 percent.

Unsuccessful letter:

Dear Parent,

At Sir Bricksmith School, we have been busy doing some really great things this year including the planning of our 50th year anniversary celebrations. Our teachers are also working really hard to make sure we achieve great academic success once again.

Did you know that Sir Bricksmith School can send you a tax receipt if you give a donation to us? We would be very grateful if you would send us a donation to celebrate all the great work we do. Just drop by the office and give a donation to the receptionist and we will get you a tax receipt in the New Year. Alternatively, you can send your donation in an envelope and your child can give the donation to their teacher.

We wish you and your family a wonderful Holiday Season and a very Happy Healthy New Year.

Sincerely,

The School Council

Successful letter:

Dear Sir Bricksmith School Parent,

We hope that you and your children have had a great start to the school year!

This year, we are taking a simplified approach to fundraising and we are offering you the opportunity to support your child(ren) by making an **annual $35 per-child donation to the school.**

With your help, we raised over $5,000 through this donation drive last year! On behalf of (School's Fundraising) Committee, I am looking forward to your continued support of this campaign.

Sir Bricksmith School parents like you have been overwhelmingly generous over the years and this generosity has helped our school and your children in many ways:

- Your children's teachers allocate at least

$100/year to enrich their classrooms by purchasing supplies, materials, equipment and/or in-class programs.

• This fund supports enrichment programs including ....

• We have made some new technology purchases thanks to your support!

• Because of the parent-led fund, the .... programs have become a unique learning opportunity for your children.

• We have purchased .... equipment for (grade) classes and sports equipment for our sports teams have been subsidized by fundraising.

• The Drama, Band, Strings and Arts programs at the school have all been enriched because of parent-led fundraising.

Please support the school and attend our School Council meetings which will give you a voice in the process of deciding where the fundraising dollars will be allocated. Alternatively, you can join an active committee or email the School Council.

To continue delivering the enthusiastic support highlighted in this letter, ***please make your donation by date, 201#.*** Thanks to your donation of $35 per-child or more, we have had the opportunity to end many of the on-going fundraising drives.

Please make your $35 per-child gift to _____ in one of the following ways:

• Write a cheque to "Sir Bricksmith Public School Council" and enclose the cheque in the attached envelope; and either drop the envelope off at the School Office or send it to the school with your child to give to their teacher.

OR

• Visit www.canadahelps.org to make a secure online donation to Sir Bricksmith School Council.

Donations over $25 will be issued a charitable tax receipt.

Thanks again for your past support and thank you in advance for your generous donation!

Sincerely,

(name)

Chair, Fundraising Committee

"When you do good in a community, the benefits eventually get back to you."

Anita Roddick

Chapter 15

THE DONATION PORTAL

If you haven't already done so, you should provide donors and supporters with a safe online portal for donations to your charity.

There are three types of online donation portals.

An externally linked web portal

This type of portal takes donors from your website to another external website where they can make a safe, online donation. This portal doesn't link back to your website but typically will send charitable tax receipts or e-receipts for you. Your charity will pay a percentage fee to cover operating and administrative costs, but, on the other hand, you'll save some administrative costs associated with receipting.

In addition to singular donations, these services may give the donor an option to make a monthly donation. Your organization should always encourage monthly giving. Not only are these your most consistent donors, but also budgeting is much easier when you can expect some stable income. Among several portals from which to choose, WWW.CANADAHELPS.ORG supports charities with small budgets in Canada by providing an external portal that can be linked from your site. As long as your organization is a registered charity in Canada, you can sign up for this service for free, but expect service fees to be deducted from donations to cover costs.

Other online portals are available; you'll need to research which one is best for your location and budget, since costs and countries covered vary. Because tax-receipting laws also vary by country, you'll need to do additional research to learn the rules in your location.

An embedded web portal within the charity's website

In this case, donors aren't aware that they are leaving the site to make their donation, and they can easily return to the website. This is because the appearance of the donation portal matches the graphic template of the website. Fees for this software vary widely. This type of software is often integrated with event management software, peer-to-peer software, and other programs used by nonprofits. It is a more expensive option initially, but it is usually worth the investment. E-receipts are also integrated with this software, saving administrative costs.

Peer-to-Peer software

Peer-to-peer software takes advantage of the basic principal of fundraising: ask for a donation and make it personal by approaching those who know you. This form of fundraising also helps enthusiastic donors reach out to their own friends and families to support a cause that is important to them.

This type of software is embedded in emails. You may have received one in the past; it's the email that arrives with a button urging you to *donate now*; clicking the button takes you to an external link that reports on the progress of the fundraiser's goals and may announce who else has contributed to the campaign. This software is often used in marathons, bike-a-thons, and cancer research campaigns. The peer-to-peer strategy is very effective because it involves individuals who encourage people they already know to support a cause close to their heart.

"You make a living by what you get. You make a life by what you give."

Winston Churchill

Chapter 16

THE TELEPHONE CALL

Telemarketing is effective in some circumstances. While somewhat expensive, it may help with long-term funding goals. The theory is that the benefit is achieved exponentially. If personal contact is made with a renewed or potential donor, the cost of the call is profitable if the donor makes a number of future donations as a result of the initial call and follow-up correspondence.

Try to recruit volunteers to call your donors (especially the lapsed donors). Recruiting volunteers is less costly and more effective. It is easier to say no to a piece of paper or an email, but it is more difficult to say no to an individual speaking directly to you on the telephone. Be very cautious when hiring professional telemarketing consultants because the costs often outweigh the benefits.

Telemarketing consultants will argue that the cost to gain each new prospective donor is an investment towards future annual campaigns and that the immediate donation is the beginning of a long-term donor relationship. This may be true in some cases. Again, volunteer recruitment for telemarketing campaigns is more cost effective. 'Do not call' legislation also requires each charity to do its due diligence. If a donor requests not to be contacted by phone, the charity is legally obliged to cease calling the prospective or returning donor.

"Men are all alike in their promises. It is only in their deeds that they differ."

Molière

Chapter 17

DINNER TIME

Knock, knock. Someone has just arrived at your door at dinnertime. Yes, the knocker wants you to make a donation to the charity the knocker represents. While the interruption may annoy you, and while door-to-door canvassing can be expensive for the organization, it is also effective, which is why it is used. Most nonprofits will need to recruit and train a team of volunteer canvassers; only the largest, richest organizations can afford to send out an army of paid door-to-door solicitors.

A volunteer team of door-to-door canvassers can be an extremely effective part of a funding strategy because the effort costs very little and the volunteers usually canvass within their own community, which takes advantage of personal connections.

Face-to-face connections with people are more effective than any other type of contact because it is difficult to turn a person away. The theory behind door-to-door strategies that use paid canvassers is that each new donor will become an annual donor without any or much additional cost, so that the upfront investment will more than pay for itself over time.

Proceed with caution when adopting a canvassing campaign. Consider costs, personal safety of the canvassers, and other important details.

*"Do noble things,
do not dream them all day long."*

Charles Kingsley

Chapter 18

GRANTING YOUR WISHES

Charitable grants from a variety of public or private institutions can bring great financial rewards. It is commonly perceived that the success of the grant is dependent upon the expertise of the grant writer. The key to writing a grant proposal, as with other requests, is to make a personal connection and/or develop a good relationship with an individual who represents the granting agency.

While writing your proposal, keep in mind the following rules that always apply:

Make a personal connection.

Thousands of charitable organizations compete for a relatively small piece of the pie. To stand out, find a way to make a personal connection to the grant-giving organization through your network wherever possible.

People give to people. Make that contact personal. Recognize that these funders are contacted daily by charities wanting money; make a positive, personal, and lasting impression when speaking to a corporate or foundation contact. If you can, make your appeal face-to-face and connect with another person in a profoundly meaningful way.

Find the funders aligned with your goals; seek champions for your cause.

Approach a corporation or foundation only when (1) your charity's mission falls within the grantor's philanthropic or strategic giving objectives or (2) you have influential contact with a senior person in the organization who will champion your cause.

To help your charity apply for grants and other funding, a number of organizations sell access to database lists that provide detailed information about foundations and corporations. With a detailed database of prospective funding partners, you can build a target list of organizations whose funding missions align with your charity's mission.

When approaching these grantors, make sure that your organization meets the criteria established by the prospective funding partner. Pay attention to deadlines and to geographic, budgetary, and reporting requirements. Personally contact the company or foundation officer if possible.

Use care and brevity in completing the application paperwork.

Proposals can be submitted to:

- Private, public, or corporate foundations

- Corporations

- Government agencies

Carefully complete whatever application process is requested by the organization and make sure your pitch matches the organization's funding objectives. Complete all questions sequentially using clear, succinct language. Lengthy explanations and extemporaneous additions to the funding application may simply irritate the reviewer. Don't waste the grant officer's time with extraneous information; that person may be reviewing hundreds or even thousands of proposals. Get to the point; this isn't an essay. Sometimes, using the language terms used by the grantor in the grant application can increase your chances of success.

With your proposal, include a basic set of materials required for most funding proposals. Have these documents readily available:

- A list of your staff and volunteer directors with an accompanying brief biography for each

- Your most recent audited financial statements

- Your most recent newsletter and/or annual report

- Your vision and mission statement

- Your most recent annual budget

- A list of your key messages or a brochure about your organization that includes the key messages

- A cover letter on letterhead outlining all contact information (postal address, email address, phone numbers, website address)

- Your charitable registration number (it should be listed on most if not all other documents in this list)

Be positive and include visuals, but don't overspend

Accentuate the positive. Discuss your organization's strengths. Make sure your proposal is attractive and use photos or charts if appropriate. Sometimes, pictures do speak more loudly than words. Some information is easier to grasp quickly in a chart rather than in text. However, spending a lot of money on your proposal could be perceived as a waste of resources.

Recognition Opportunities

Highlight recognition opportunities that are available to the granting institution. Recognition opportunities are often an important factor in your proposal. Examples of recognition opportunities are:

Media: Newspaper or magazine advertisements, lists of sponsors on websites, newsletters, brochures, flyers, event programs, maps.

Physical: Naming of buildings, rooms, and wings of buildings, paintings, benches, trees, wall plaques, chairs, bricks and more.

If your proposal is successful, congratulate your team. Make sure to follow up with proper stewardship practices. Call and send a receipt and/or letter of acknowledgement within twenty-four hours of receiving the funds, deliver reports on time, respond to queries for information regarding the organization's donation or sponsorship within hours, recognize the funder's support using whatever methods were promised (on the web, on signage, at events, etc.), and continue an open dialogue with the organization.

If you aren't successful, don't give up. Remember that 80 percent of your revenue will come from 20 percent of your sources. This theory recognizes that, while most of your proposals will be rejected, those that support your work will more than make up for those letters of rejection. You have to find that 20 percent that will give you your main support.

"Corporations have neither bodies to be punished, nor souls to be condemned; they therefore do as they like."

Edward, First Baron Thurlow

Chapter 19

THE CORPORATE PHILANTHROPIST?

The guiding lights of the corporate marketing machine would like you to believe that businesses very generously support the charitable sector; however, before you accept that, consider the facts.

In Canada, corporate funding accounts for $1 billion of philanthropic revenue annually. However, the lion's share of donations goes to a small group of charities. According to Imagine Canada's Research Bulletin No. 13-2, which looked at charities with annual revenue exceeding $1 million, 84 percent of corporate donations went to only 7 percent of those charities.

Know the rules of engagement when you're dealing with the corporate or private business sector:

Corporations rarely make donations and/or sponsor events for purely altruistic reasons

When you make your pitch, tell corporation representatives how your charity will provide marketing and promotional opportunities for corporations that donate; from the corporate viewpoint, answer that classic question: What's in it for me?

In addition, the company will consider each sponsorship or donation as an investment and will look for a return on that investment expressed in measurable results, such as number of people served by a program, number of performances, number of meals served, number of people attending an event, or number of victims sheltered.

Connections count

Many companies have a policy of funding organizations where their employees volunteer. If you have an existing relationship with a donor, volunteer, or director who works for a company that supports charities similar to yours, be sure to involve the contact when drafting and delivering the proposal.

For example, if a director is a manager at a Bank, ask the director to personally make contact with the sponsorship or donations officer within the company to discuss the proposal. Personal contact may mean the difference between success and failure. It is not a guarantee for success, but it increases your chances.

Matching means doubling donations

Make your donors aware that some corporations will match employee donations. Encourage your donors to find out if their companies will match their contributions to your charity.

Turn allocations into receipts

The United Way will allocate gifts to your charity if a contributor requests that directed giving. Make sure your charity actually receives the donation. Directed gifts could be reallocated if follow-up is neglected or if donation records are inaccurate or incomplete.

Rise above the crowd

Yes, your charity does wonderful work, but keep in mind that you are competing with thousands of other charities for the same dollars. One bank executive recently reported to a fundraising colleague that in 1990, the bank received about 50 requests for funding each week. In 2012, the same bank received more than 1,000 proposals each week. If the bank donates to 500 charities each year, your charity has a small chance of being successful—unless you increase your chances by establishing a strategic connection to that company.

Identify natural partnerships

Try to find natural partnerships to support your organization. For example, if you are raising funds for a charity helping the blind, a natural corporate partnership would be any company that sells products or services related to sight (glasses, laser eye surgery, contact lens solutions, sunglasses).

"What we have done for ourselves alone dies with us; what we have done for others and the world remains and is immortal."

Albert Pike

Chapter 20

SHOULD WE APPROACH FOUNDATIONS?

Foundations are a good source of revenue for many charities; however, many foundations will grant charitable agencies only once every few years. You will rarely find granting agencies that are interested in financially supporting annual operating expenses. Make sure you understand the difference between public, private, and corporate foundations. Understanding these differences will help you approach them for financial support.

Private Foundations

Private charitable foundations set up by individuals and families provide estate tax havens for them and financial support for the charitable sector. However, investment incomes have fallen to a historical low as a result of low interest rates. As a result, private foundations have had fewer resources to distribute to charities during the past couple of decades. The donation policies of private foundations vary. A subscription to foundation directories can help you understand the individual nature and requirements of these foundations. Some foundations will accept funding applications and some will not. Foundation directories available in Canada include Imagine Canada's Directory of Foundations, available via the Imagine Canada website.

Revenue Canada requires Canadian charitable organizations to file T3010 charitable tax returns annually. By studying a foundation's T3010 return posted on Revenue Canada's website, you can gather information about the foundation's assets, board of directors, and past funding recipients. This database treasure trove is a free resource.

Public Foundations

Public foundations are quite different from private foundations and are defined differently, at least in Canada. Their boards and disbursement rules are different. Public foundations are generally set up as public endowment funds to support directed charitable initiatives. Public foundations nearly always publish websites, hire staff to manage the foundation, and require charities to comply with lots of complicated and competitive application procedures.

If possible, make personal contact with a foundation's staff and work to develop a relationship with the grants officer. This can give you a competitive advantage. Comply with requests and make sure your mission is a good fit with the foundation's philanthropic or program policies. Remember, other charities will be more appealing to the foundation if your organization is not a good fit: in this case, you can't fit a round peg in a square hole. It simply won't work, and you will be wasting your time.

Again, consider your competition and try to build a relationship with the foundation's personnel. This will increase your chances but by no means will it guarantee financial support. Again, if someone in your organization knows senior-level foundation staff or directors, that person should make the contact. Personal contact is very relevant in this highly competitive field.

Corporate Foundations

Corporate foundations are set up to direct philanthropic funds from a corporation to the charitable sector. Usually, an employee or a team of volunteers within the company will make decisions about where funds will be allocated. All of the rules of engagement that apply to public and private foundations apply to corporate foundations as well.

"Thousands of candles can be lighted from a single candle, and the life of the candle will not be shortened. Happiness never decreases by being shared."

Buddha

Chapter 21

CAPTIVATING YOUR AUDIENCE

If you want to build enthusiasm and directly engage and captivate your supporters, organize an event. Some organizations rely mostly on event-based fundraising while others are afraid to take the plunge. Fundraising events, no matter how big or small, are very labor-intensive and require a very organized leader/coordinator and a strong volunteer committee.

The benefits of event fundraising go beyond the revenue. Events build a sense of community, create awareness of the charity's work, and engage individuals or companies in a tangible, unique way. Events can be as small and low-cost as a series of garage sales or lemonade stands or as large as a walk or bike-a-thon involving tens of thousands of individuals.

Including the coordination of an event in your diversified funding model can help establish a more secure revenue stream and may bring you closer to your most important advocates. Events offer positive and memorable experiences to participants, a profoundly important gain if your organization is interested in developing long-lasting, supportive relationships with its donors.

Some companies support charities only through event sponsorship, and some individuals are interested in supporting charities by bowling, golfing, running, or biking. Make sure your charity uses this event as an opportunity to engage with its participants in the most effective way possible. Deliver a consistent message that is emotionally charged and provide your audience with an opportunity to volunteer, receive additional information, or donate with ease.

Review this advice before you start:

Consider that every event is an opportunity to meet with prospective and current supporters face-to-face.

• Most events raise the majority (80 percent) of their funds through sponsorship opportunities, including programs, signage, beverage sponsors, and prize sponsors. Sponsorship revenue usually meets or exceeds the cost of organizing the event.

• Communicate with every participant before, during, and after the event.

• Keep your dialogue consistent by using your key messages. Present your mission and vision at the event. Keep your presentations strong, emotionally charged, and BRIEF. Don't invite individuals to an event and then expect them to sit through an hour of speeches during a dinner reception. A short, powerful speech is more effective than a series of long-winded speeches.

• Events are labor-intensive; make the work fun and recruit enthusiastic, energetic volunteers to help out.

• You need a committee of volunteers to help staff coordinate the event.

• Don't forget about clean-up. Everyone likes organizing events, but people seem to disappear when it's time to clean up. Appoint a crew in advance for that chore.

• Make use of the web and integrate your

messages with social media, your website, and through peer-to-peer software for pledge-based campaigns.

- If a prospective participant backs out because the date or time of the event is not convenient, ask for that person's support to subsidize someone else and allow another participant to attend without paying the entrance fee.

- Be careful if using a 'headline' act. Have a contingency plan in case your scheduled performer becomes ill or is called away to an emergency.

- Have a weather contingency plan in place where appropriate.

- Make sure to consider security, money management, and event insurance.

- Award your volunteers with a meal or a reunion after the event.

"By failing to prepare, you are preparing to fail."

Benjamin Franklin

Chapter 22

THE EVENT PLAN

Stick to the five W rule to cover all aspects of planning an event. While real estate is about location, location, location, event planning is about details, details, details.

Who?

Who will attend the event? Who is your target audience? Who will participate? If you are featuring a celebrity, have you thought of what you will do if the celebrity can't attend? Do you have volunteers to help you coordinate the various aspects of this event? Who might be willing to sponsor/pay for the costs involved in organizing this event?

Where?

Where will the event take place? How much will it cost? Do you need to cater the event? Will there be enough parking? Is the event taking place inside or outside? Do you have a plan to deal with inclement weather? Where will you advertise or promote this event?

When?

You need to establish the event date and start and end time, but before setting that date, think about how much time will be required for before-the-event steps, and allow enough lead time. Consider what other events might be happening at the time you want to schedule your event; avoid competition that can cut attendance.

What?

What type of event will you organize? What is the sequence of activities to take place before, during, and after the event? What specific sponsorship opportunities can you offer to potential sponsors? Book your venue well in advance of the event.

Why?

Why are you coordinating this event? If this is a fundraising event, what is the financial goal?

Make sure that all communications surrounding this event state who, what, where, when, and why. I have seen too many posters for events that omitted the time or date of the event ... a costly error indeed.

Feed and water the volunteers – important details

Make sure you develop a detailed checklist before coordinating your event. Think of everything you need and everything that needs to happen in sequential order. Remember to feed and water the volunteers because they are there to help and support your cause and deserve to be treated with respect. Volunteers are often an overlooked resource. The task of coordinating an event will become easier and easier once you recruit a committed group of volunteers who return to do their job annually.

Finally, remember safety, sanitation, and comfort requirements. Contact the organization's insurance provider to make sure the event is insured. Mentally walk through how participants will be spending their time: are there enough toilets so attendees don't miss the start of the race or performance? Is there a garbage detail and supplies? How will recyclable material be handled? What image of your organization will participants have if garbage cans are overflowing or runners are passing out from lack of water stations?

Be creative, enjoy the process, and always remember to think about the mission of the organization when things get tough. You are there to help, and in the helping, you will find ample reward.

"The essential element in personal magnetism is a consuming sincerity – an overwhelming faith in the importance of the work one has to do."

Bruce Barton

Chapter 23

THE POWER OF PERSONAL CONNECTIONS

Do you feel the sweat upon your brow? Do you get nervous when you think about asking a friend, family member, colleague, or neighbor for money? Do you imagine feeling rejected or embarrassed? This fear can stop you and your colleagues from asking for the donations that your charity needs. It's normal to not want your ideas, passions, and efforts rejected, but overcoming a fear of rejection is necessary if you want to help your organization succeed in its mission.

These suggestions can help you deal with negative feelings when asking for a donation:

Participate in a workshop and practice asking a potential donor for a significant donation.

Practicing (role playing) will help prepare you for the real scenario. Remember the reason you are involved with the charity before entering into a discussion about it. Remember that you are reaching out to ask others to support something you believe in. You are asking the individual to support the charity, not to support you personally.

Remind yourself that you are not asking others to support a charity that you haven't profoundly supported yourself. Note: if you haven't made a significant donation to this charity (within whatever means you possess), you are unlikely to be successful in asking others to donate. Always make this commitment before asking others to do so. Sincerity, integrity, and passion are the keys to a successful charity fundraising campaign.

Define what you will request. Do you want this individual/company to sponsor a program, a capital campaign, or a scholarship?

- **Be prepared.** Have a materials package available that includes:

- An audited financial statement

- An annual report

- Organizational brochures, newsletters, pictures

- Operating and/or program budget figures

- A written proposal

- Contact information

- Charitable registration number

- A brief video presentation if you have one

Always ask for a donation in person wherever possible. The more personal you make the pitch, the better. If you can't meet face-to-face, try to talk on the telephone or, better yet, via an online video communications system such as Skype. Letters and emails might work; however, face-to-face communication is, without doubt, the most effective method of fundraising.

If you are going to write a letter to a prospective donor seeking a major gift, handwrite the letter or handwrite a personal note at the bottom of the letter. For instance, you could add this note to a letter:

Thanks for attending the art auction last week. I hope to see you again soon. Please support .... charity; it means the world to me.

Tips for meeting with prospective donors:

Begin the meeting by briefly discussing something personal you have in common to create a warm, comfortable initial connection.

Thank the individual for taking the time to meet with you.

Start the discussion about the charity by making an opening statement similar to this:

"I have made the commitment to volunteer my time on the Board of Directors (or other committee) of >>>>> charity."

It is important for the prospective donor to know that you have nothing personal to gain by supporting this charity and that your request comes from your heart.

Talk about why you have made this commitment and briefly highlight the wonderful work the charity has done lately as you show the individual the charity's background material. You might start by saying:

"The mission and vision of this charity mean so much to me because ….."

Discuss the reason(s) the charity is reaching out to others to gain financial support (for instance, increased need, new program, a loss of government funding, capital campaign).

Ask the prospective donor if he/she would be "willing to support the XXXXX campaign with a gift of $_____." It is important to specify a targeted amount of money to demonstrate the need and to give the individual prospective donor a benchmark.

Be prepared to discuss recognition opportunities, such as naming buildings and publicizing the donation on the nonprofit's website or in its newsletter. Such recognition often appeals to the prospective donor, and the chance to memorialize a lost loved one or promote a business through a naming opportunity can be appealing.

Offer optional forms of payment (i.e., a $10,000 gift can be paid in four $2,500 installments over the next two years).

Place a fully detailed, written proposal in front of the prospective donor.

If the prospect declines the offer, leave the proposal and ask him/her to review it for future consideration. Make a plan to get in touch at a later date. Ask if the prospect would consider volunteering with the organization.

If the prospective donor agrees to support the charity with a generous donation, thank the contributor and make sure that you and the organization's staff stay in touch with this individual and follow up by sending a personal note of thanks, providing promised recognition opportunities, and keeping the donor up to date on your charity's activities.

What to do when a prospective donor agrees to make a substantial donation:

Celebrate, call the donor immediately, cash the check, send the charitable receipt out within 24 hours, and write a personal note of thanks. Stay in touch with the donor, respect recognition agreements, invite the donor to all events, and invite the donor to volunteer.

"When you are grateful, fear disappears and abundance appears."

Anthony Robbins

Chapter 24

RELATIONSHIPS TAKE TIME TO GROW

Create an environment based on gratitude and don't forget to thank, inform, and secure a strong, trusting bond with the donors who are generously supporting the charity.

A stewardship policy must be drafted, adopted, updated, and above all, put into practice. A policy is useless unless all staff and volunteers are aware of it and make a serious commitment to adopting it. People give with their hearts. If major donors don't feel that generosity is appreciated, they will discontinue their support in the future and possibly damage the reputation of the charity among their own peer network.

All too often, I have witnessed serious administrative errors such as careless misspelling of a name in the database. Don't be the executive leader who neglects to call a donor in a timely manner after receiving a significant gift. The donor who makes a major gift must be treated with respect and gratitude.

Neglecting or disrespecting donors can result in profoundly negative, costly consequences. Make sure you take the time to send out thank-you letters, speak to significant donors, and nurture those who are financially supporting your charity. Cherish those who make the charity's work possible.

Pay attention to your correspondence with your donors at every level. If the donor has moved, find the resources (volunteer, if possible) to ascertain their new address. This might take some time and a little sleuthing; however, it is important to do so.

Pay attention to names, dates, addresses, email addresses, and other data and keep accurate records of whatever details you possess about each donor. This will allow you to segment your donor list properly. For example, if you are coordinating a women's fashion event, make sure you can segment your list to determine which of your donors are women. Pay special attention to donors who have been regular supporters. Your loyal, long-term donors are most likely the key to sustainability.

Consider your competition

No matter what your organization accomplishes, hundreds if not thousands of other organizations are accomplishing similar goals. Evaluating your competition can strengthen your goals by showing you best practices used by other organizations. While many methods can help you research your competitors, these two will help you research the detailed reports available to you for free:

As I have mentioned before, a free database resource is open to all Canadians. The tax returns of all charitable organizations are published on this site. To find the site, use the search terms "Revenue Canada + charities listings"; I have provided search engine keywords rather than a link because links often change. These listings name directors, source(s) of revenue, and more. It provides a great snapshot of each charity. In the United States, the IRS no longer provides online public access to the tax returns of registered charities. This is not surprising, since over one million charities exist in the USA.

Examine the websites of your competitors and browse through the information relevant to fundraising. What type of events do they coordinate? Who are their sponsors and funders? Do they receive government funds? Who are the directors and volunteer committee members? Read annual reports if available and look for links between their board and donors.

Remember that what works for other charities may or may not work for your organization. Sometimes their sponsorship list will give your organization a clue as to which companies are willing to support similar areas of philanthropic work, and sometimes the sponsors are involved solely because of a personal connection to someone in the organization.

"Creating channels between people who want to work together toward change has always been one of the ways that social movements push the world forward and make it better."

Mark Zuckerberg

Chapter 25

SOCIAL MEDIA & ONLINE CONTENT

Social media is extremely popular these days, and hundreds of companies are touting their skills as 'social media specialists.'

On its own, social media occasionally provokes direct donations to your charity. Social media should be defined as an extension of your ongoing public relations strategy. All communications, including social or traditional media, can contribute positively to your efforts to communicate your mission and vision.

The charity's website must be included in this 'integrated' communications plan. A number of factors should be put in place while designing your web engagement strategy:

• Your website should contain attractive visual cues and links.

• Your website should link to your blog and all social media pages or channels.

• The design should be kept simple and easy to navigate.

• Your design must work for those using a cell phone as well as a computer.

You needn't worry about specializing in social media, since your communications with the outside world, including your donors, friends, colleagues, is fundamentally social. You will shape your message to cater to differing demographic audiences, whether Facebook page, Twitter account, blog, and other social media portals. Twitter requires brevity; a blog can be more expansive.

Once you have captured interest, you can ask for support, but first emphasize your work. All communications, including social media, must be consistent with your mission and vision. Be careful in choosing who delivers these your organization's social messages. Social media puts your organization under the microscope.

Having said that, to have an impact, your organization must issue regular (at least once a day or week) messages through all social media outlets because some messages will be missed or not delivered. For example, if you tweet, followers not on Twitter at the time might miss your message. Scheduling messages when they are most likely to be seen by your audience can boost exposure.

Relevant and interesting messages are more likely to be read. Test to find out what works for various audiences. Your Facebook group will probably not be the same audience as your Twitter, Pinterest, and other groups. Make sure to use relevant #hashtags and 'keywords' to grow your audience.

Monitoring how often a message is re-tweeted (Twitter), Pinned (Pinterest), and shared (Facebook), (Instagram) is a way to determine which messages are most effective. Testing everything will improve your communications plan. Monitor audience feedback and questions (such as Comments or Messages on your charity's Facebook page) and interact when appropriate.

In a crowded marketplace, it is important to communicate on a regular basis using a variety of media including print, social media, and email. Integrate your social media messages with your direct solicitation practices. This integration will provide the recipient with an opportunity to learn about your work and then make a donation. Don't expect social media to bring a surge of donations. Having 200,000 Facebook fans isn't necessarily an indicator of wide financial support. It simply indicates a lot of Facebook fans.

The reason your organization should use social media is to drive people to your cause and to help you grow your community of supporters. Social media helps your organization deliver useful, provocative information to your community. A well-organized social media campaign 'integrated' with your direct communications can be effective because each individual has an opportunity to share an interest in your organization with his or her own personal contacts. This sharing may or may not lead to raising more funds.

Social media is a powerful communications and public relations tool and a great way to keep your audience involved and enthusiastic about your work. Make sure to use imagery and integrate a call to action.

Example of social media integration plan/web content strategy:

Charity A is going to organize a nationwide BBQ event. Planners want their most loyal donors and supporters to participate by coordinating their own personal fundraising barbecue event on May 15. This date marks the birth of the charity's founder.

Here's a small sample of an integrated communications strategy. The sum of the parts will strengthen the campaign as a whole:

December 15

Announce barbecue event in direct mail piece and on the website.

March 1

Send direct mail letter to donors; include a newsletter or insert announcing the barbecue event. Acknowledge the major sponsor on printed materials.

March 1

List the event on Charity A's website and open registration.

March 5

Post a message on all social media sites (Facebook, Twitter, Instagram, Pinterest,

LinkedIn, YouTube etc.) announcing that invitations have been mailed and registration is open for an exciting new BBQ event.

March 15

Announce an early bird contest or other promotion for the barbecue event to pique interest. Post this announcement on the website, on all social media channels, and to the internal email list.

March 15

Send a media release to local media outlets across the country where donors are hosting events.

April 1

Post a 'we're not fooling around' reminder announcement to social media outlets and the email list encouraging participation and reminding participants of the contest deadline.

April 30

Announce winners of the barbecue event contest; deliver social media messages and email notices.

May 5, 10, 11

Use all web and social channels to deliver enthusiastic announcements to remind participants of the event. Announcement should be personal (a good story, a recipe, the number of others who have signed up for the event).

If you have purchased person-to-person or peer-to-peer software, a personal message from one individual to another is often a great way to spread the word about an event or a campaign. Include a link to create an actionable response within the email or social media announcement. This software can easily be integrated with your campaign.

"No one has ever become poor by giving."

Anne Frank

Chapter 26

THE PLANNED GIVING LEGACY

Planned giving is a complex topic that requires its own book to explain, and many such books are available; this chapter is merely an overview. Planned giving allows charitable organizations to secure a more stable financial future. These gifts often provide tax benefits to the donor as well and are often significant for the charity.

It is wise for your charitable organization to find allied professionals who can explain the best options for your donors. Allied professionals include insurance brokers, trust and estate officers, lawyers, accountants, financial planners, and other professional advisors.

Planned gifts include:

• bequests

• gift annuities

- charitable remainder trusts

- residual trusts

- life insurance policies

Along with making sure professionals handle the legal and taxation complexities of planned giving, you need to develop a strong, personal relationship with the donor. The donor who plans a gift feels passionately about the mission and vision of your organization, and your program will benefit most if a representative of the charity personally visits with the prospective donor and discusses a variety of options to strengthen the financial health of the charity. One very successful planned giving officer I know put it this way:

"A great planned gift is discussed over a cup of tea in the kitchen or living room of the prospective donor."

Make sure the donor and the charity have received professional advice before arrangements for a large planned gift are finalized.

"Generosity is giving more than you can, and pride is taking less than you need."

Kahlil Gibran

Chapter 27

THE VOLUNTEER BOARD

Great leadership is difficult to find. In Canada, charities cannot pay their directors; all board directors are volunteers. Some of the charities I have helped have had their share of leadership challenges. The board of directors plays a very significant role in the charitable sector, and I cannot emphasize enough that the directors must be engaged without being micromanagers, must have a succession plan in place, and must lead all strategic planning and implementation. In the charitable sector, success is not measured by profits, but by the charity's ability to fulfill its mission and vision.

The board of directors must be the positive light that guides the team. They represent the conscience and the soul of the organization. They must willingly be the ambassadors who care deeply about the mission and vision of the organization. If this isn't your Board, I suggest you begin a process to search for those individuals who will help your charity fulfill its mission and vision.

Organizations use a variety of methods to find volunteers. Here is a brief list of suggestions:

- find a local volunteer network and advertise your volunteer position(s)

- advertise for volunteers on your web site and social media channels

- ask your existing network of volunteers for suggestions, introductions

- do a web search of business leaders who have shown an interest in your area of expertise

- advertise in local print media

- check to see if local TV stations coordinate volunteer listings

- contact various human resources managers in your area to enquire about volunteer network possibilities

Treat the volunteer recruitment process like a paid employment position and interview potential candidates. Your organization will be more successful if the scope of the position including expectations and responsibilities is clear from the beginning.

The board of directors is legally responsible for the charity. New directors should be provided with a training session and a board manual, and all directors should have a clear understanding of what is expected of them.

A final word of advice: have fun and enjoy the journey!

RESOURCES

Here's a short list of resources you can use to further your understanding of fundraising:

www.imaginecanada.ca

http://www.afpnet.org

www.charityvillage.com

www.charityinfo.ca

Revenue Canada Charities Listings:

http://www.cra-arc.gc.ca/chrts-gvng/lstngs/menu-eng.html

ACKNOWLEDGEMENTS

I didn't choose fundraising as a profession. Fundraising fell into my lap. My personal journey began when I was hired to help an organization with a national peace campaign. The temporary part-time position blossomed into a twenty-year fundraising career. Fundraising is best illustrated as an emotional rollercoaster because one experiences an abundance of celebrations and disappointments along the way. I want to thank my editor Pat Bray for helping me deliver a clear message and Kerry McLorg for helping me with the layout. Thank you , David McHale, for supporting me throughout this journey, and Sophie and Lauren, for being the magic in my life. Thank you to my mentor, friend, and sister Judy Stanleigh for encouraging me to write this book. I also thank Allan Stanleigh, as a writer and a great resource, and because he has always been there for me. Thanks to Sheena Lambert, David Windeyer, Anne Kerr, Fiona Chapman, Howard Bloom and many, many others for hiring me and believing in my skills. Thanks to hundreds of wonderful staff and volunteers I have worked with throughout the years. You have made my fundraising journey a success, and this book is dedicated to my time spent with you.